Fooling Ewe

www.FoolingEwe.com

Library of Congress Control Number: 2013931664

ISBN: 978-0-9889019-0-2

Published by Service Bar Books

www.ServiceBarBooks.com

Printed in the USA

1st Edition

Did you know "Ba-a" can mean anything, even "Thank you"? Ba-a to Kickstarter and Ewe backers like Kevin Kelly, Al Tambolleo, Rob Mayo, Jared Marcus, Nate Cross, Dennis Curtis, and Sarah Anderson Ba-adway. To Marcia Stone, Mike Zonghetti, Craig O'Donnell, and Hopkinton Pediatric Dental. To Westborough Orthodontic Associates, Tim DeMello, Jamie Lambert, and Jonathan Slawsby. Ba-a Cindy Curtis Callisto and Todd Ba-a, I mean Galusha. Ba-a Steve Thibodeau, Chris Himmel, and James Ball, and ba-a Anthony at Blick. Ba-a Matt Tompkins for coloring me and ba-a very much to all of you who make cookies! Mm, and #LoveEwe -Ewe

Thank you to all my friends and family whose encouragement was unwavering. Todd Finklestone who gave Ewe a face, Matt Tompkins who gave Ewe hue, and Shaun Bamforth who gave Ewe things to do. Thank you Lisa Jahn-Clough, my teacher and friend, who watered me when I was just a seed of a writer. Dale Demers and Steve Thibodeau, my mother and brother, who watered me when I was just a seed of a man. Bob Demers and Rob Thibodeau, my father and brother, who continue to water my soul from Heaven. And my daughter, Adelyn, who waters my life. This is for you. -Mike

Thanks to the whole Ewe flock (Mike, Matt & Shaun). This is for my students in Bamenda and Belo- keep up the great work; the staffs, volunteers, and supporters of CameroonONE & RUDEC; my brothers and sisters at ShelterBox who every day deliver shelter, warmth & dignity to people made homeless by disaster worldwide; my mentors from Suffolk EPP for blessing me with eudaimonia; and Marcia, Don and the rest of my friends and family. -Todd

Fooling Ewe

Ewe grazed the grass today.
Ewe grazed the grass yesterday.
Ewe grazed the grass every day because
"That's what ewes do," said Ewe's mother. "All alone, from dawn 'til dusk."

But Ewe did not want to graze anymore.
Bored in the meadow day after day, now Ewe wanted to play.

So Ewe went to the chicken coop disguised in feathers.

"Cluck cluck cluck," Ewe clucked. "I am a chicken."

"That's just clucky!" said Chicken.

"Ha ha!" Ewe laughed. "I fooled Chicken!"

And to the pig pen caked in mud.
"Oink oink," Ewe oinked. "I am a pig."

"Want a bath?" said Pig.
"The mud is nice and dirty."

“Ha ha!” Ewe laughed. “I fooled Pig!”

And to the lake wearing summer squash like a beak.

"Quack quack," Ewe quacked. "I am a duck."

"Okay," said Duck. "I'll paddle with you."

"Ha ha!" Ewe laughed. "I fooled Duck!"

Ewe was having a wonderful time. Until Mother showed up.

"Back to the meadow, Ewe, and graze that grass," she said. "Grass won't graze itself, you know."

And back to the meadow Ewe trudged.
But when Ewe spotted the cows,
Ewe couldn't resist.

Ewe put on spots and sneaked to the pasture.

“Mooooo,” Ewe mooed. “I am a cow.”

“A dairy cow?” asked Cow.

“Ha ha!” Ewe laughed. “I fooled Cow!”

And went to the pond wearing lily pads.

"Croak croak!" Ewe croaked. "I am a frog."

"Greaaat,"said Frog. "Let's chase flies."

"Ha ha!" Ewe laughed. "I fooled Frog!"

And went to the cornfield and stood perfectly still.

"I am a cornstalk," Ewe whispered.

The corn didn't say a word.

"Ha ha!" Ewe laughed. "I fooled Corn"

Ewe was having even more fun than before. Until Mother returned.
“Get grazing,” she said. “Don’t make me say it again.”

Ewe trudged back to the empty meadow to graze. But then she spotted the barn.

"Neigh," Ewe neighed, with hay draped over her neck. "I am a horse."

"I like your mane," said Horse. "It's fancy."

"Ha ha!" Ewe laughed. "I fooled Horse!"

And she crouched beside a mouse hole
holding the garden hose like a tail.

"Squeak squeak," Ewe squeaked.
"I am a mouse."

“A big one!” said Mouse. “Want some cheese?”

“Ha ha!” Ewe laughed. “I fooled Mouse!”

And she put on a straw hat and overalls and...

...knock knocked on the farmer's door. He answered with a cookie in his hand.

"I am a human," Ewe said. "May I have that?"

Farmer's mouth opened but nothing came out.

And Ewe waited patiently for one, two, three seconds, and then *snatched* the farmer's cookie and stuffed it in her mouth.

"Ha ha!" Ewe laughed. "I fooled Farmer!"

Ewe was having the time of her life.

Until...

...Mother Ewe shouted, "That's it! You're grounded!"

But, to her surprise, the meadow was now full.

"Mother," Ewe said upon seeing the meadow now full of "ewes", "There are plenty of ewes to graze the grass. You don't need me."

They dropped their disguises and there was Chicken, Pig, Duck, Cow, Frog, Horse, and Mouse.

"Ha ha!" all the ewes laughed. "We fooled Ewe!"

Ewe laughed and they laughed and, after they helped Ewe graze the grass, they all played in the meadow.